The J

CW00566075

S Gallagher

BookLeaf
Publishing

Presentation by *BookLeaf Publishing*

Web: www.bookleafpub.com

E-mail: info@bookleafpub.com

ISBN: 9789395026741

First edition 2022

DEDICATION

For anyone who has ever struggled.

ACKNOWLEDGEMENT

To the people who have been with me through all the breakdowns, emotions and lowest of lows. Thank you for standing by me, for all the words of wisdom and mostly for loving me through it all.

Clogged Arteries

There is a cigarette in place of were my heart
should be,
but everyone is trying to quit these days.

The Lazy River

The sharper the knife, the deeper the cut, the closer to death.
I don't feel a thing.
See the blood and I am numb, see the blade and I laugh.
I've become addicted to the release.
The blood... The most I feel alive.

Nostalgia

I'm feisty.
I'll stand up for myself.
People know I have their back,
I'll scream and scrap for them.
So why when it mattered am I silent?

He throws his fingers where no one has been
before.
He claws the blood from complete pain. I'm not
pushing him away?
No screaming.
Instead, I pray.

I stood weak. Afraid. I was only child.
My innocence torn away in minutes.
This is the reason I fight now.

Overthinking? My Specialty

The loneliness consumes me.
The only company I have are the voices.
They tell me my flaws.
Reasons I am alone.
What happens when even they leave me?
How can silence be so loud?

(Un)Conditional Love

"It's just a shock. It'll take some time. Just don't
tell anyone yet. How do we explain it?"
They say a parents love is unconditional.
So why do I never feel good enough?
Why can you not tell your friends about me?
I am comfortable in my own skin, I am happy, I
am me for the first time.
That doesn't seem to matter.
You are ashamed of me so you remove your
love.

Your Big Duck

The guilt consumes me.
What if I don't see you before it happens?
Will you recognize me even if I do?
How do I live knowing I didn't get to say
goodbye?
Will you ever know how much I love you?
Going back changes my life forever,
staying hurts my heart forever.
But no disease will take the memories.

One is the Loneliest Number

You made me laugh till I felt abs.
Our private jokes, forgetting about the busy
crowd.
Now I'm Crying alone instead of comparing our
depressions.
How do you get over a best friend?

Soulmates

I don't make friends easily,
people have never really understood me.
We met in hell and god handed me a piece of
heaven.
I knew it, when I ranted through an ugly cry and
saw nothing but concern.
After all who says soulmates can't be found in
friendship?

Pretence of Love

He begs you not to go.
Says you can't leave him.
Screaming he needs you.
Pleads he loves you.
The worst kind of love,
a convenient kind.
He does not know you so he cannot love you.

Searching for Home

How long can you miss something for?
I crave the belonging of where I call home.
I cling to the people.
Surround myself with flags, pictures, follow
silly little superstitious myths.
People don't understand my voice here.
I run home to the motherland to find,
people don't understand my heart here.

Don't Speak

Tell me your secrets you beg of me.
Will you love my flaws? I need you to.
Own my soul?
Don't judge what has been done to me, love who
I am standing in front of you.
Trust my heart I beg of you.

Light at the end of a Bumpy Road

I try to smile through the pain.
I'm fine.
I keep repeating, I'm fine.
So why do I feel like I can't breathe?
I feel numb but my head is working overtime.
My heart is feeling everything.
I am overwhelmed by darkness but then,
Then I see your light.

Escaping Reality

One hug made me loose my mind.
One kiss made me loose my soul.

The Window

My parents warned me about drugs,
they forgot to warn me about the eyes I would be
addicted to.

Holding all of You

You tell me stories about your childhood.
You tell me the names of your family. (I'll never
remember)
Laughing when I say words in your language.
Crying with memories of your childhood.
I want to hurt them how they hurt you. Instead,
I curl you up with me and love the parts you hate
the most.

The Only Way I Know How

She stood there crying, looking at me for
answers.
I start rambling making things worse.
How can you question my love for you?
I grab you and let you feel my love.

Sunday Baths

Repetition, it never stops.
Over and over.
Feeling like no way out.
You are my escape,
Always different.
Always magic.

This is Me

How does he see me now? I'm not that 14 year
old girl anymore.
Is he scared I will tell someone or laugh at me
because I never have?
Does he hate me or regret what he has done to
me?
Do I ever even cross his mind?
It doesn't matter.
I love the woman I am today.
I've fought like hell to become her!